NEW YORK, EMPIRE CITY

NEW YORK, EMPIRE CITY 1920–1945

DAVID STRAVITZ

WITH AN ESSAY AND CAPTIONS BY CHRISTOPHER GRAY

HARRY N. ABRAMS, INC., PUBLISHERS

SHERRY-NETHERLAND, SAVOY-PLAZA,
AND THE PLAZA HOTELS
seen from Central Park

To Amy and Alison

New York had all the iridescence of the beginning of the world.

—F. Scott Fitzgerald, "My Lost City," 1932

In the late 1970s I was developing a series of special effect photographic filters and I became hooked, and I mean *hooked*, on photography. I began shooting around New York City with old large-format cameras—2¼ x 3¼s to 4 x 5s and 8 x 10s. Many of the lenses of the 1930s produced spectacular results. Some were a bit soft and warm, and others were tack sharp and contrasty. Working with a view camera made me understand the flexibility of this instrument—how marvelous it is in correcting converging parallel lines, a limitation of even the most expensive single-lens reflex cameras today. When you think about the difference in the size of the negative between, say, an 8 x 10 camera and that of a 35mm camera, you can begin to understand how large you can blow up an image without the image breaking up and losing sharpness.

A fellow photo enthusiast who lived in New Jersey called me to let me know of an aerial photographer who was closing his studio and selling his equipment. Hoping I would come upon some great equipment, I jumped into my car and appeared at the photographer's doorstep. A gruff, rather frail-looking elderly gentleman opened the door and I walked into his darkened studio, which had the strong smells of over thirty years of darkroom chemicals. By the time I arrived, the pickings appeared to be slim, however I did select two large-format cameras, an old tripod, and a few studio lenses, making it already worth the trip. As I continued to poke around a bit more, I discovered some boxes stacked in a darkened corner of the room. "What's in these five boxes?" I asked my host. "Just some old stuff, no lenses, no cameras— just negatives." "Hey, I collect images also—may I take a peek?" "Yes, but I've already arranged to reclaim the silver from them." I later learned that it

was a common procedure then for photo labs and professionals to send their no longer needed negatives to a reclaiming service.

I moved the five boxes squarely under a light and proceeded to open them one by one. The smell was overpowering—residue from silver nitrate and Kodak safety films, chemicals, decomposing reticulated images, and crusty old manila envelopes. It was impossible to review all the images then—there turned out to be around 500 total—but I bought the whole lot. When I returned to New York, I discovered I had purchased an important lost piece of New York history—images of New York City and the surrounding suburbs, all taken by people whom I believe were working for the photographic team of Alfred E. Peyser and August L. Patzig.

These urban pioneers of architectural photography created *masterpiece*s under difficult and complicated circumstances. The professional photographer who produced these negatives using an 8 x 10 camera likely dragged seventy-five plus pounds of gear around with him, including tripod, camera, lenses, sheet film holders, blackout cloth, and a ground glass loupe. Setting up one shot might take a few hours to accomplish. Since many of these spectacular images are taken from high floors of nearby buildings, it likely took hours, if not days, to get approval, drag the gear up, set up the shot, take the shot, and fold the equipment back into its cases. Professionals working with expensive sheet film would likely shoot three exposures, bracketing from slightly underexposed to normal to slightly overexposed. If something went wrong, it was a major undertaking to go back and re-shoot.

Among the images I found are photographs from the construction of the Chrysler Building, a broad assortment of views of other famous and not-so-

HOTEL LINCOLN
Eighth Avenue, 44th-45th Streets

famous buildings, ballparks, and the 1939 New York World's Fair—simply work-for-hire assignments. Many of the manila folders had markings on them, such as "$10 to XYZ Company for one-time use in XYZ article or publication." Some seem to have been used many times over by different people and others by just a few. And yet, even so, these images of New York, taken by masterful architectural photographers from the early 1920s through the late 1940s, are nothing short of spectacular. Not only do they show great skill in manipulating the same equipment used by such masters as Ansel Adams, Margaret Bourke-White, and Berenice Abbott, but they also show us the vibrancy of New York at a moment of incredible excitement.

An obscure New York City guidebook of 1939 called *New York, The Giant City,* by Laura Spencer Porter, compiled by the Travel Bureau of the Woman's Home Companion, sets the scene for the images in this collection, providing a brief history of New York to the late thirties tourist: "In 1636, ten years after the Peter Minuit bargain, the first small permanent Dutch settlement, called New Amsterdam, was finally established on Manhattan." The pamphlet goes on to say "But that early Dutch city extended only as far as what is now Wall Street. Beyond that—nothing but wilderness and beasts."

In the early days, when the little old town from which New York sprang reached only as far as what is now Wall Street, where a wall or stockade was built for protection against the Indians, it belonged to the very small group living within its limits, some 500 souls in all. In the 100 years during which it belonged to the English, its popu-lation increased to 30,000. This was the size of the town when Washington in 1789 took his oath there as first President of the Republic. It had grown to the North until it reached what is now City Hall Park. In 1939, 150 years later, it has increased until its population is something over 9,000,000.

The guidebook also outlines some of the "Outstanding Facts about New York for Those Who Like Statistics." Here are some of those facts, which I'm including in this compilation because the timeline of these images pairs closely with the data from the pamphlet.

It is the largest city in the world in area at 309.84 square miles. It is exceeded in population by one city only—London. New York has more skyscrapers than any other city in the world—close to a hundred of them, of thirty stories or more—with a valuation of *about* $800,000,000. It has more buildings over 500 feet high than exists in all the other cities of the world put together. "As far back as 1929 the Superintendent of Buildings reported that New York had enough electric elevators to carry 105,000,000 persons 78,500 miles daily." That is roughly the current population of Mexico transported around the earth three times daily.

The Empire State building is the tallest building in the world, 102 stories. It has in it seven miles of elevator shafts. It has over 6,000 windows; a floating population of 40,000 a day; and enough floor space to shelter a city of 80,000.

Porter goes on to state that the New York park system is the greatest and its water system is the most generous, providing 145 gallons per day per inhabitant, versus the 43 gallon allowance provided for residents of London.

SAVOY-PLAZA HOTEL
east side of Fifth Avenue, 58th–59th Streets

It has more and greater bridges than any other city, built at the following approximate cost: Brooklyn Bridge, $21,000,000; Williamsburg, $25,000,000; Queensboro, $25,000,000 (including land); Manhattan, $24,000,000; Hell Gate, $14,000,000; Blackwell's, $29,000,000; George Washington, $60,000,000 (the third largest suspension bridge in the world (3,500 feet); Triboro, $60,300,000.

In 1937, before the Lincoln Tunnel existed, we had only the Holland Tunnel.

The Holland Tunnel is one of the most famous tunnels in the world and the greatest under-water tunnel. It was 7 years building. It is 9,250 feet long. Of *this* span 5,480 feet are under water. It has twin tubes each 31 feet wide, sunk to a depth of 75 feet under water. It was used by 12,446,284 vehicles in 1938.

In 1939, "Trinity Churchyard, at Broadway and Wall Streets, in which lies buried the author of *The Night Before Christmas*, is the most valuable churchyard in the world. The land is estimated to be worth $25,000,000." And "The R.C.A. Building in Radio City has the largest floor area of any building in the world, 2,924,036 square feet. It has more visitors than any other business building, 80,000 a day." "The Rainbow Room on the sixty-fifth floor is the highest night club in the world, with a more magnificent view than any other."

Porter goes on:

New York has a larger food and marketing list than any city in the world. In 1937 it received and marketed the following:

Butter	220,662,677 pounds
Eggs	206,419,720 dozen
Cheese	61,302,749 pounds
Milk	1,449,331,480 quarts
Cream	61,212,400 quarts
Dressed Poultry	206,602,823 pounds
Live Poultry	164,592,200 pounds
Meats	1,595,785,926 pounds
Fruits and vegetables	4,714,752,000 pounds
Fish	500,000,000 pounds
Total in Pounds	10,965,059,176 pounds

The New York Main Post Office is the largest in the world. Fifteen million letters pass through the New York Post Office each day; about 300,000 pounds of newspaper and periodicals, and 72,000 insured C.O.D. and parcel post packages.

In this book you will experience rare images of a city that began as New Amsterdam from a $24 purchase by Peter Minuit 300 years ago, and 100 years after the invention of photography by Daguerre. What amazing progress in so young a city. New York was then, and still is, the Empire City, and I am pleased to have the good fortune and opportunity to share with you these wonderful images taken over seventy years ago.

—David Stravitz

OLD McGRAW-HILL BUILDING
northwest corner of 36th Street and Tenth Avenue

There is something . . . BIG about these photographs, miraculously rescued by David Stravitz two decades ago. I don't mean big in size, although certainly they are that: enlarged from the original 8 x 10-inch negatives, they capture detail like gold dust. No, it's a bigness of scope, of ambition, of vision—reflecting and reflected by the city and the time they document.

Recall the works of Timothy O'Sullivan and others documenting the American West in the mid-nineteenth century. These photographers faced down astonishing hurdles, transporting chemicals, crates of glass plates, and their own supplies by wagon and mule and their own backs to remote areas in Colorado, Nevada, and other states, as distant from their own civilizations as the moon is from ours.

They—and we—were rewarded with sweeping views of an essentially foreign country revealed in astounding detail, and a sense of sublime majesty of the American West.

As the western frontier was closing in the early twentieth century, Alfred E. Peyser and August L. Patzig were beginning their photographic careers in New York. Peyser was born in New York to German-born parents; Patzig was born in Germany about 1895. Of their training, outlook, social status, and other issues we know nothing. They incorporated their company in 1924 with $15,000 in capital. Their credit line appears occasionally in newspapers and architectural journals of the period, and sporadic listings in directory sources reveal little about their specialty. It is possible that they did not actually make all of "their" photographs: photographers such as Ewing Galloway evolved into picture agencies, with other photographers working for them under contract.

What could it mean that Margaret Bourke-White and Peter Juley chose to be listed under "Photographers—Commercial" in *Polk's New York City Directory* of 1933, but the firm known as Peyser & Patzig chose—along with Edward Steichen and Irving Underhill—simply the "Photographers" category? Probably nothing.

Peyser & Patzig will always be known for an astonishing series of construction photographs of the Chrysler Building, as it rose from an excavation to a stainless steel pinnacle; they must have produced scores, perhaps hundreds, of other such records, all lost, or at least lying fallow, uncollated in a myriad of photo collections.

The large-format view camera had been the gold standard in picture-making in the nineteenth century, particularly for architectural photography, but new technology in the 1920s and 1930s made the small-format film camera feasible, and new photographic movements were making it logical—after a time, the big box cameras came to seem like dinosaurs, introducing formality and rigor compared to the supposed naturalness and spontaneity of more casual machines.

By the 1920s the precisionist view of cities was falling out of favor, replaced by that of the "artistic" photographers—who interpreted rather than documented—even though many of the latter continued to use large-format equipment. Alfred Stieglitz's grainy, indistinct photographs of the Flatiron Building were typical of this new vision—with gauze over the lens, you didn't need high definition. Whether by temperament or training, such artistic baggage was clearly anathema to Peyser & Patzig, who lugged around a giant box camera with crates of sensitized glass, painstakingly setting up carefully composed views for even the most average

NATIONAL BROADCASTING BUILDING
665 Fifth Avenue

of buildings—down to a Queens intersection and even a vacant lot in the Bronx.

But both their subject matter and their scrupulous clarity left them in a deepening, low-status hole of utilitarianism, like realist and classical painters after Abstract Expressionism swept the art scene. For some reason the expansive western photographs of the nineteenth century are still considered elevating, while their urban corollaries are simply . . . functional. I suspect that far more Deep Important Motives have been imputed to O'Sullivan et al. than they possibly could have had time for on the trail.

So, do Peyser & Patzig's photographs have anything to say to us, besides the mere recording of detail, an archaeological dig not in Nineveh or Luxor, but merely in our own backyard? According to conventional histories of photography, no, they are just ASCII files, plain text to the high art of more interpretative photographers.

I see it differently.

Look at the late 1930s view south past the Cathedral of St. John the Divine, as broad a vista as any mule-borne photographer witnessed. From left to right it sweeps over the construction scaffolding of St. John the Divine, then still billed as the largest Cathedral in the world, its planned spire a last gasp of urban optimism. It passes from the Central Park reservoir to the pyramid of the Carlyle Hotel, the Chrysler, RCA, and Empire State buildings; past downtown skyscrapers near the future site of the World Trade Center and the New York Bay, which Hudson sailed three centuries before. It's an architectural panorama of the American century.

In this picture, Peyser & Patzig have chosen as their foreground the architectural plankton of the city, the anonymous five- and six-story tenements and flats that held the vast bulk of the city's population—who worked in and even built the skyscrapers. These littler buildings are like the Navajo on horseback in Edward Curtis's famous nineteenth-century view of the Canyon de Chelly cliffs—the micro dwarfed by the macro. On their roofs, the mark of human habitation—underwear, socks, and towels—drying in the breeze. Each one was clipped to the clothesline by an invisible human hand—just like the ancient inscriptions on the Newspaper Rock in Utah. They flap in the breeze, like a campfire suddenly deserted, with a coffeepot still bubbling.

Not all is deserted—on a few towels, actual inhabitants! One is sunbathing on the tar beach, another around the corner in a chair—each unaware of the other. You don't have to think that this is an image of the alienated condition of modern man to be moved by it. Both figures are also unaware of but still bathed in the complex panorama of the city, a perspective privileged to the photographer and viewer.

Photographers like Peyser & Patzig are often derided because they were "in business"—but most photographers—even Robert Mapplethorpe—are in business. Art is frequently, perhaps usually, a byproduct of commerce, and Peyser & Patzig were no different. Many pictures were made for specific clients, usually of specific buildings, and were paid for by the architect, the limestone supplier, the engineer—anyone who needed a picture to demonstrate their own accomplishments. The architect William Van Alen was very definitely in business, but that does not compromise the worth of the Chrysler Building.

Examine the photograph of the Pythian Temple on West 70th Street, built in 1928. The subject, a wild, Egyptian-style Masonic lodge, is hard to photograph, a massive, tall building on a narrow side

FEDERAL OFFICE BUILDING

ENERAL FLAVORS INC

BRITISH EMPIRE BUILDING
630 Fifth Avenue

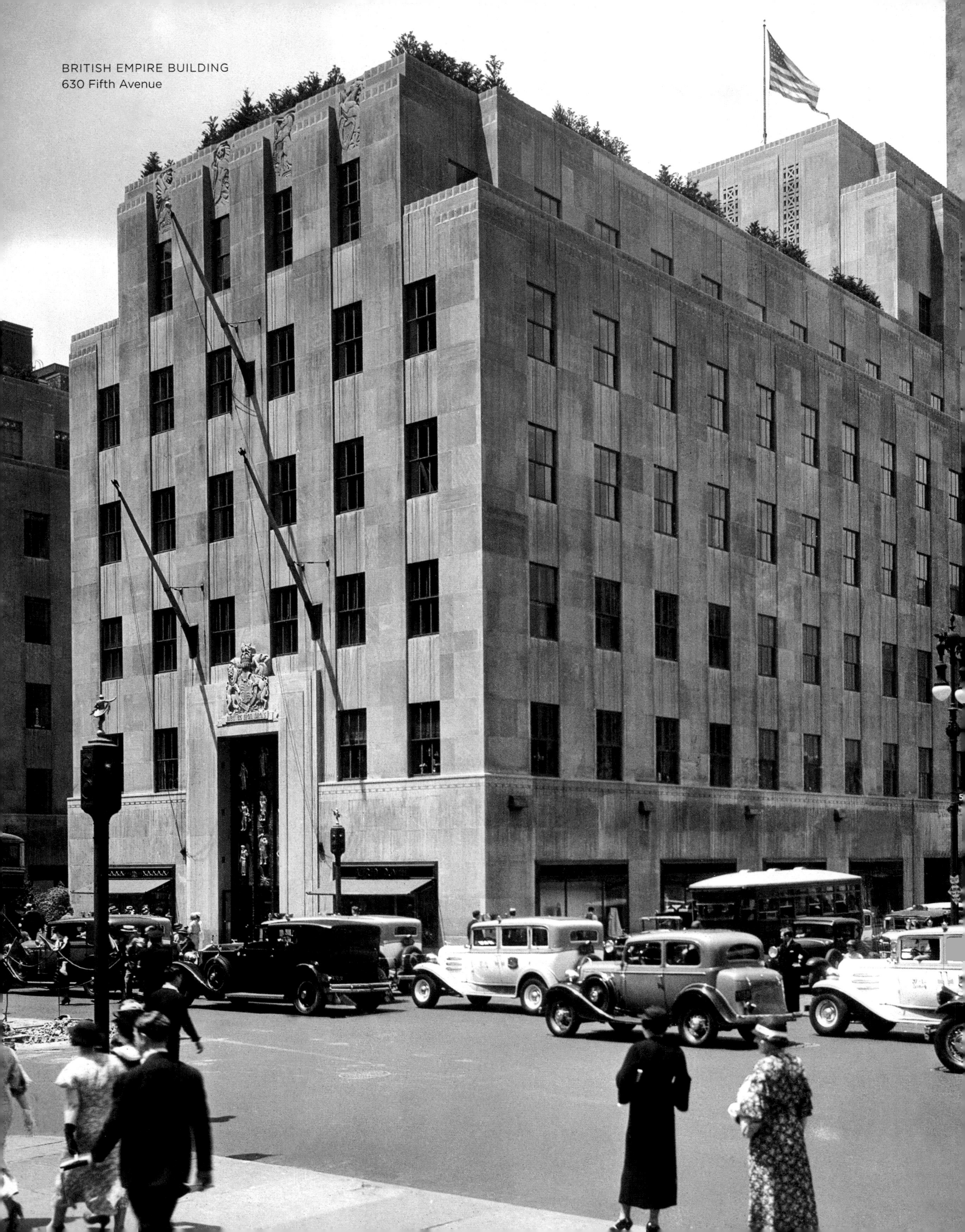

street. By expanding the frame to left and right, and putting the building to the left of center, Peyser & Patzig were depicting—in the context of a straight urban photograph—the collision between the nineteenth and twentieth centuries then going on, from the old brownstones to the new setback skyscrapers.

Since the return of Precisionism in the 1970s with painters like Richard Estes, the mediated image—where a subject must be "interpreted," and where the simple depiction of reality is considered insufficient of serious attention—has lost its former primacy. But architectural photography has not rebounded on the same scale—an elite few still work in large-format cameras, but publishing protocols and economy have dictated that the typical photograph of a building today is from 35mm film (or, worse, an even lower resolution digital photograph), perfectly suited to carry the brittle minimalist architectural ambitions of post–World War II architecture but, optically, a tragedy.

In many of these photographs, it is possible to see immediately commercial motives: the images of the new Post Office on Church Street, the Daily News Building, the Panhellenic Tower are, apparently, documentary records of the structures as they first appeared. Probably someone paid for these photographs directly.

But then there are other images which appear straightforward, but . . . well, they leave an itch in your mind. Of what possible use is the image of the 1939 World's Fair subway station? It's not for a magazine: there are no people in it. It's not for the architect: way too much barbed wire! OK, maybe it's for the designer of the rocket-fantasy light pole, juxta-posed against the Trylon—but how do we explain that there are far more of the older 1920s light fixtures in the photograph. How could anyone really "use" this photograph? Likewise, the photograph of the fairgrounds actually captures only a few of the fantastic modern designs of the exposition whose theme was "Building the World of Tomorrow." Mostly the picture is about . . . a nearly empty highway. About asphalt! The commercial value of such a photograph is hard to see.

Consider the intense scrutiny of the billboards of Ebbets Field: just what were they doing there, and why did the client—if there was one—need it recorded on giant silver nitrate negatives? Wouldn't, perhaps, something more modest have sufficed: a photographer using 4 x 5- inch film negatives or even . . . a Leica?

Perhaps they were just careful. Perhaps they were discreetly "artistic." Perhaps, in some photographs, they were just having fun. But Peyser & Patzig left a view of America's Empire City with a vast sweep, an urban "big sky country." We don't know what portion of their work this collection represents, although it must be a small one. We don't know whether these images survived because they were chosen or because they were just in the right part of the attic to escape disposal. They are hardly, as they survive here, systematic or thematic—indeed, were the partners to return they might pitch most of them out.

But Alfred Peyser and August Patzig did leave a broad, inspiring, intoxicating vision of the greatest city in the greatest country in the world.

—Christopher Gray

NEW YORK CURB EXCHANGE
78 Trinity Place

THE TOMBS
100 Centre Street

THE JOSEPH HILTON & SONS BUILDING
northeast corner of Fulton and Nassau Streets

BEAVER BUILDING
82–92 Beaver Street

West Side improvement, looking northwest towards the Merchant's Refrigerating Building at the southwest corner of 17th Street and Tenth Avenue

PARK AVENUE HOTEL
west side of Park Avenue from 32nd to 33rd Streets

WISELY ENTER
WITH US TO LAY FOUNDATIONS
YOUR OWN MONEY·REWARDED
FOR THE YEARS TO COME

·INGS·BANK

Looking south on Broadway past the old
Herald Building, 36th to 35th Streets

PERSHING SQUARE BUILDING
southeast corner of 42nd Street and Park Avenue

SIXTH AVENUE EL
33rd Street station

Final Chrysler Building scaffolding

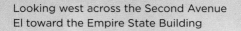
Looking west across the Second Avenue
El toward the Empire State Building

DAILY NEWS BUILDING
42nd Street and Second Avenue

BARCLAY-VESEY BUILDING
140 West Street

NEW YORK LIFE INSURANCE BUILDING
northeast corner of Madison Avenue and 26th Street

East on 42nd Street from the Chrysler Building

Southwest from the Chrysler Building
while under construction

East side of Fifth Avenue, 53rd to 54th Streets

364 Broadway, northeast corner of Franklin

1 Fifth Avenue, southeast corner of 8th Street

North on Fifth Avenue, past the Waldorf-Astoria

THE UNION CLUB
northeast corner of 51st Street and Fifth Avenue

SAKS FIFTH AVENUE
northeast corner of 50th Street and Fifth Avenue

The last of the Vanderbilt mansions, northwest corner of 51st Street and Fifth Avenue

43 Fifth Avenue, one block north
from Washington Square Park

HOTEL PRESIDENT
234 West 48th Street

PRINCE GEORGE HOTEL, interior

HOTEL PRESIDENT, interior

AMBASSADOR HOTEL
northeast corner of Park Avenue and 51st Street

HOTEL BELLECLAIRE
southwest corner of 77th Street and Broadway

FRED F. FRENCH BUILDING
551 Fifth Avenue

RAINBOW LOUNGE
30 Rockefeller Plaza

Prometheus in the sunken garden,
30 Rockefeller Plaza

Looking north on Broadway, past the
Times Building at 42nd Street

CHRYSLER BUILDING
basement room

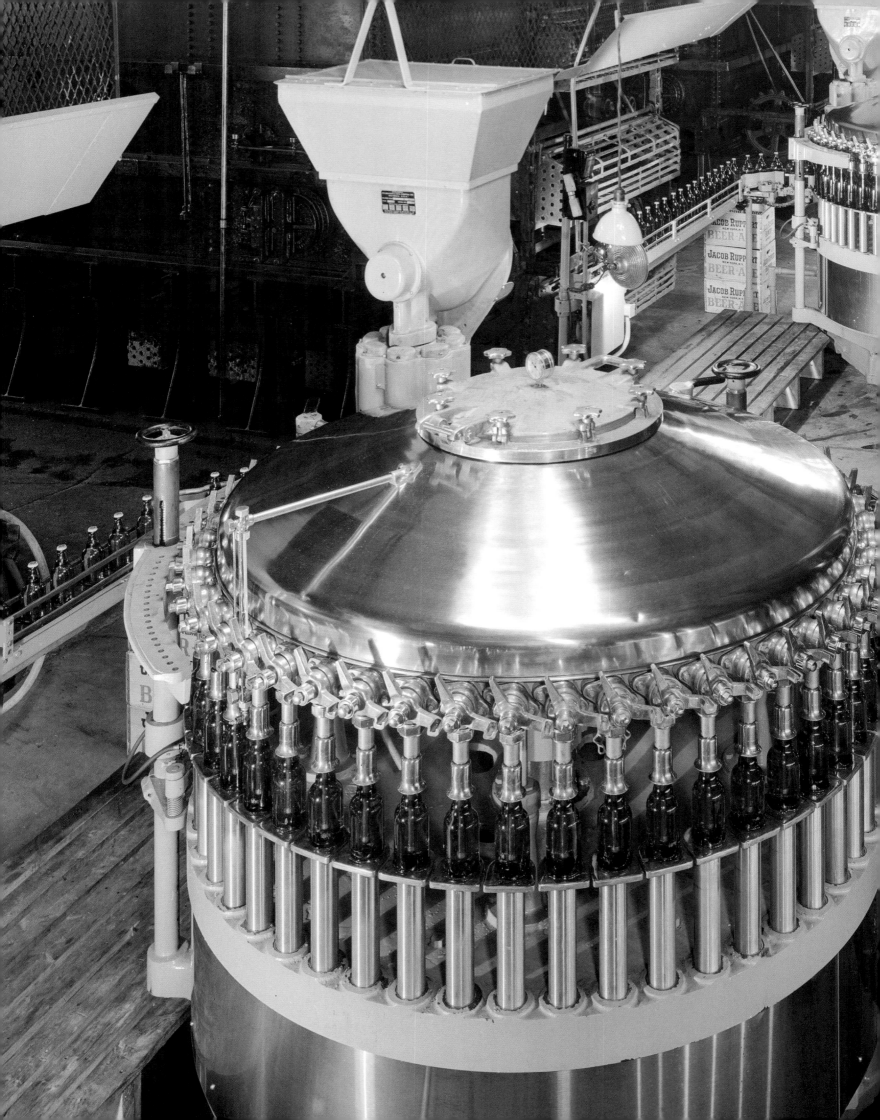

RUPPERT BREWERY
probably the Yorkville plant, Third Avenue and 91st Street

FISK TIRE BUILDING
250 West 57th Street, from
Broadway to Eighth Avenue

AMERICAN RADIATOR BUILDING
40 West 40th Street, seen from Bryant Park

THE KNOX BUILDING
southwest corner of 40th Street
and Fifth Avenue

Looking northwest from the Chrysler
Building to the New York Central Building,
230 Park Avenue, at 46th Street

Miller Highway, south across
the rail yards at 72nd Street

South past the Cathedral of St. John the Divine, from 113th Street and Amsterdam Avenue

West Side Highway docks

French luxury liner Normandie

PANHELLENIC HOUSE, groundbreaking ceremony

PANHELLENIC HOUSE
northeast corner of 49th
Street and First Avenue

PANHELLENIC HOUSE, terrace

1939 NEW YORK WORLD'S FAIR

125th Street, Lexington Avenue to Third Avenue

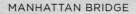

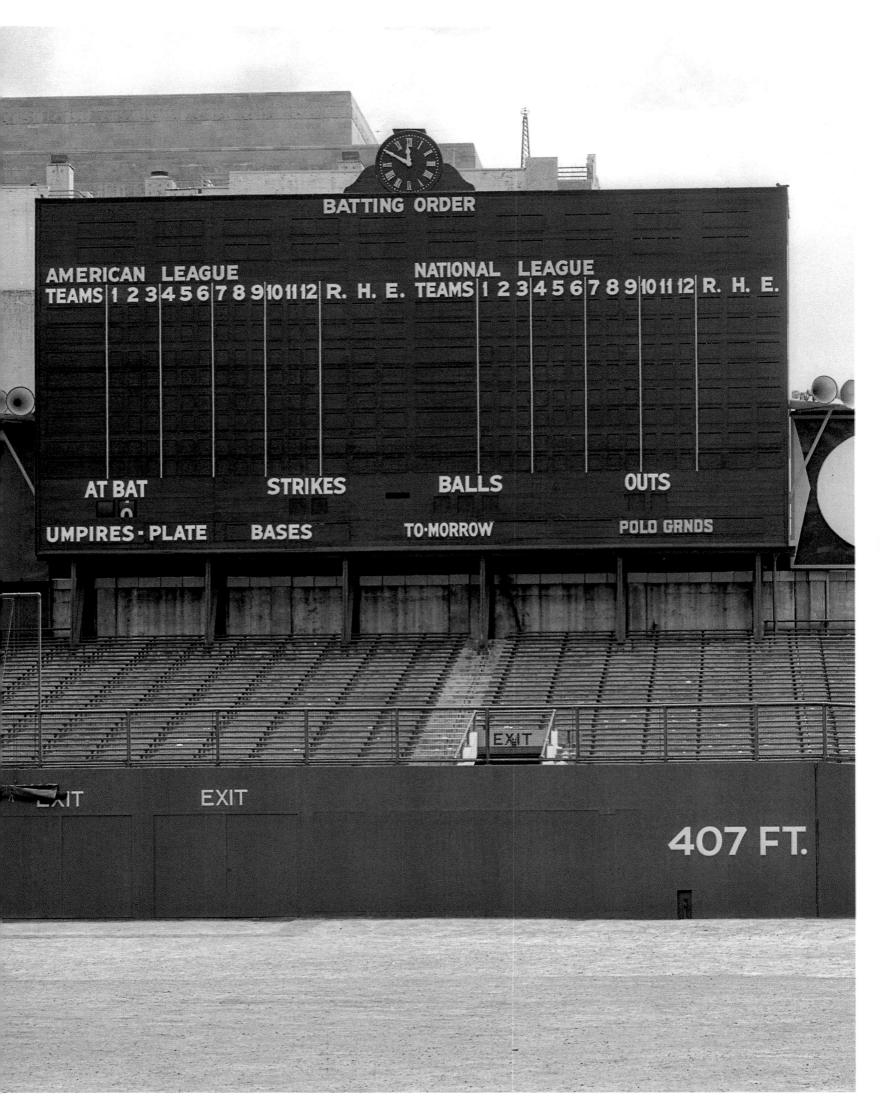

EVERY FRIDAY

CORN EXCHANGE BANK
TRUST CO.

74
NEIGHBORLY
BRANCHES

ESTABLISHED 1853

MEMBER
FEDERAL
DEPOSIT
INSURANCE
CORPORATION

FOR A
LONG DRIVE

TYDOL
A

FLYING A
GASOLINE

KOPPER OUTDOOR ADV. CO.

ASK ANYBODY

414 FT.

447 FT.

Intersection of Broadway and 138th Street

Southeast corner of Broadway at
134th Street

Midblock view, from Forest to Tinton Avenues,
between 163rd and 165th Streets

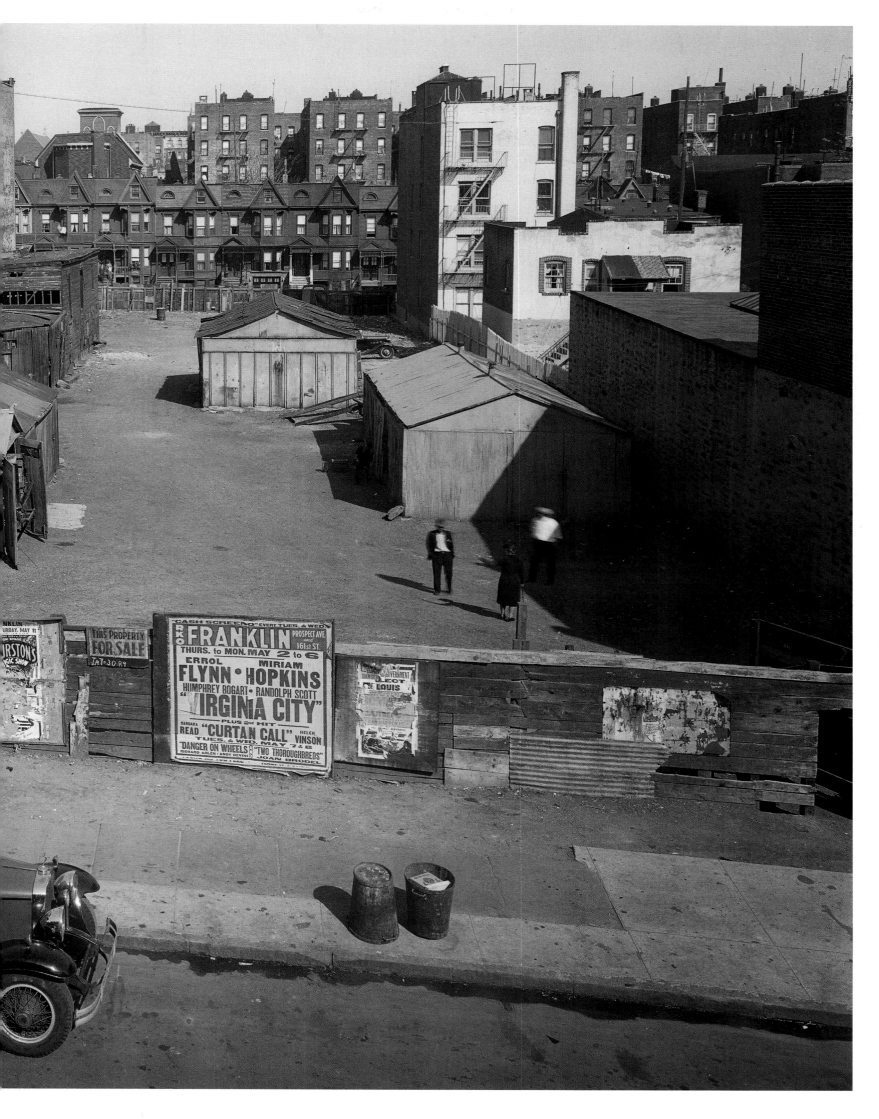

Midblock view, from Forest to Tinton
Avenues, between 163rd and 165th Streets

Coney Island bathhouses

The Boardwalk Cafe at Jones Beach

Coney Island beach and jetties

Coney Island beach, boardwalk, and bathhouses

Page 6
The Architects' Building, 101 Park Avenue

This 1913 building was, on the inside, New York's architectural bazaar. Architects hoped that owners would prowl the halls looking for talent, but of course the prowlers were really materials salesmen with catalogues of bathroom fittings, terra cotta, cast plaster ornaments, and other things. This was the home of Kenneth Murchison, Arnold Brunner, and other firms, like McKim, Mead & White, which remained here from 101 Park's opening until its dissolution in 1961.

Plain modern boxes are now out of fashion, but 101 Park Avenue poses an interesting question: what is it that makes up the "traditional architecture" which we now so esteem? This building has a limestone ground floor, some terra cotta decoration near the corners, and a few minor cornices and balconies. But 90 percent of the surface is as plain as a warehouse. It is peculiar that the 10 percent balance, really a trifling amount, can now make the difference between architectural heaven and hell. One possibility is that we look through a filter which favors old things, and that this neo-Renaissance style building is really not as far from utilitarian modernism as we think.

Page 9
Hotel Lincoln, Eighth Avenue, 44th–45th Streets

The trade journal *Decorative Furnisher* said the interior of the 1928 Lincoln was the first large building in the United States to be done "in the modern style"—with heavy use of geometric Art Deco styling. But the exterior was purely commercial architecture, "American twentieth century," said the magazine *Edison Monthly*. Such dichotomy is common in New York City, where the full exteriors of high rises often cannot even be seen from the street, and where the architectural personality of a building is seen as residing on the inside.

Page 10
Savoy-Plaza Hotel, east side of Fifth Avenue, 58th–59th Streets

Built in 1928 for the developer Harry Black, the twenty-nine-story Savoy-Plaza was a late, tepid design by McKim, Mead & White. But it was grand, and helped define the space of Grand Army Plaza, arguably New York's most successful public square, ringed by the Squibb Building, Bergdorf-Goodman, the Metropolitan Club, and the Plaza, Pierre and Sherry-Netherland Hotels—which were all generally white or beige. The *W. P. A. Guide to New York City* of 1939 praised the "extraordinary unity" of the surrounding buildings.

Sixty-somethings and tiki-tiki aficionados know it as the original location of Trader Vic's, purveyor of Fogcutters, Po-Po, Cho-Cho, and other exotic foods, with outriggers, spears, grass roofs, and other Polynesian decoration overhead.

Alas, the 1960s saw the ascent of Hilton-tacky in hotel design, and the thick walls, elegant spaces, and solid materials of the 1920's hotels seemed drastically old-fashioned. Thus, when an investment group came down the pike in 1964, the hotel owners checked out—with no tip. In October, the architects and teachers Elliot Willensky and Norval White—who had picketed the demolition of Penn Station—organized their students in a demonstration at the Plaza to protest the demolition of the Savoy-Plaza. Signs included "Renege on Rampant Wrecking," and one placard, "Landmarks Preservation Weak," was a bitter satirical jab at Mayor Robert F. Wagner, who had just declared "Landmarks Preservation Week" but had not put the proposed landmarks law into effect. One student, Miles Kurland, carried a sign "Save the Seagram Building"—he told the *New York Times* he was "thinking ahead."

This picket line was insignificant compared to the one at Penn Station, and did even less—the Savoy-Plaza was demolished for Edward Durell Stone's pretty-awful-but-not-as-bad-as-it-could-be fifty-story General Motors Building, a proto–World Trade Center of Georgia marble columns and a setback sunken shopping plaza, the result of a zoning bonus. "A sick planning joke," wrote Ada Louise Huxtable in the *New York Times* in 1966—the plaza not only broke the building line surrounding the real plaza, but also the sunken aspect created a pedestrian scar in the landscape. The introduction of the plaza bonus was one of those mid-century iconic benefits which were, according to a unanimous orthodoxy, supposed to save the city. It did not. Here was a case where we had all the open space we needed, and in 2000 the developer Donald Trump covered it over.

Page 13
Old McGraw-Hill Building, northwest corner of 36th Street and Tenth Avenue

This bright, white terra cotta–sheathed factory building is a cut, perhaps several cuts, above the competition of the time—no wonder architects like Gwathmey Siegel, Richard Meier, Sam White, and others have located there in recent years.

Designed in 1913 by Starrett & Van Vleck, this was at first the "Hill Building"—Hill Publishing became McGraw-Hill Publishing in 1917. With three-quarters of the facade area given over to glass, and sixteen-foot ceilings, it is an astonishing place to enter for those used to the usual dank loft buildings, more like an airport terminal than a warehouse. The sparkling high-mindedness of what was essentially just a factory was a good omen—in 1930 McGraw-Hill hired Raymond

Hood to design its successor building at 330 West 42nd Street, a landmark in New York modernism.

Page 17
Federal Office Building/Post Office, 90 Church Street

This WPA limestone extravaganza, with its modern classic ornament and stylized eagles, has lovely, robust art moderne interiors in the post office section. This "Federal Moderne" style has come to be associated with the patriotism of Franklin Roosevelt's brave vision for America.

Page 18
British Empire Building, 630 Fifth Avenue

At near left, one of the elegant "Mercury" light poles of 1929, designed by Joseph H. Freedlander, with streamlined detailing, red and green lights, and a gold-leafed figure of Mercury on the top. The first was installed in 1931 at 41st Street and Fifth Avenue, and 103 more followed on Fifth from 8th to 59th Streets.

In the late 1950s the city began to replace them, and only three of the original 104 Mercury figures are known to survive. The disposition of the other 101 has never been established—it is hard to believe that they were junked, but at the same time no others have surfaced. Their disappearance marked a downward slide into supposedly utilitarian uniform stoplights and streetlights from which the city is only now beginning to recover.

Pages 20–21
New York Curb Exchange, 78 Trinity Place

This is the classic shot of the contradictorily named institution—how can a curb exchange be inside a building? But it did meet on Broad Street—or rather, in Broad Street—from the 1860s until moving to Trinity Place. This view across the gravestones, suggesting the hollowness of financial gain, was a frequent theme for mid-century photographers; perhaps they lost a lot in the crash of 1929.

Pages 22–23
The Tombs, 100 Centre Street

Harvey Wiley Corbetts—who imagined dense skyscraper cities—here produced his prototype building in the form of a magnificent high-rise penitentiary, a ziggurat of (they hoped) correction. Go down to the courtroom proceedings sometime, preferably with your impressionable children who are considering a life of crime. The scene is actually of a lost underclass of petty offenders whose lives are so shattered they are beyond hope.

Pages 24–25
The Joseph Hilton & Sons Building, northeast corner of Fulton and Nassau Streets

Built in 1928 as a department store, only a decade later the Joseph Hilton & Sons Building had descended to "Special Merchandise Left Over N. Y. World's Fair . . . At A Great Sacrifice." The Art Deco gargoyle gutters and the austral window transoms (horizontal outswing panels which offer better circulation, rain protection, and cleaning access than do most others) show that the architect, B. Robert Swart, was thinking.

At the right stands the venerable Keuffel & Esser company, drafting instrument makers—the facade is decorated with compasses and other drafting equipment, barely visible to the right of the "Billiards" sign.

Chock full o' Nuts, the ground floor tenant, was the Starbucks of its day.

Page 26
Beaver Building, 82–92 Beaver Street

New York's brutal grid plan discriminates against these lovely little urban triangles, but this one, designed by Clinton & Russell, has survived in the crazy quilt of the Wall Street area.

Page 27
West Side improvement, looking northwest towards the Merchant's Refrigerating Building at the southwest corner of 17th Street and Tenth Avenue

Although the surface freight railway (at first called the New York and Hudson Railroad) up the lower West Side predated residential buildings by half a century, the surface rail line's nasty habit of running over women and children (or running over working men, and leaving widows and orphans) raised enough of a stink to raise the tracks above street level on a massive steel viaduct, with spur connectors into the relevant industrial buildings. Now disused for a quarter century, a nonprofit group is working to take it over as an urban park, which they are calling the High Line, and a walk down through the weeds sprouting between the wooden ties is indeed a transporting experience. The current owner, CSX, would also be transported because they are otherwise required to pay the cost of demolition. But, once fixed up, it will never have the same decaying, ghostly majesty it does now.

Pages 28–29
Park Avenue Hotel, west side of Park Avenue from 32nd to 33rd Streets

Built in 1869–78 by dry goods merchant A. T. Stewart as a women's hotel, the Park Avenue Hotel was meant to be a wholesome environment for the new generation of independent female office and factory workers who otherwise had to put up with possibly immoral boarding houses. The great experiment failed; the cast iron structure became a regular hotel within a few years.

Pages 30–31
Looking south on Broadway past the old Herald Building, 36th to 35th Street

Note that the "Building Coming Down" and store closing signs are posted only on the west side of the building, which was demolished in two sections. This Florentine fantasy was designed by Stanford White for Herald owner James Gordon Bennett, Jr.—the view through the ground floor windows of the running presses was a wonderful sidewalk show, especially because you could take it in after the theater or opera along this stretch of Broadway.

Page 32
Pershing Square Building, southeast corner of 42nd Street and Park Avenue

The Pershing Square Building and the Bowery Savings Bank, which is adjacent to it, were designed by architects York and Sawyer. Pershing Square was built in 1923, in one of the fastest growing areas of Manhattan—midtown. The building was outstanding for its time, with most of the other neighboring buildings still consisting of four-story leftovers from the late 1880s.

Page 34
Final Chrysler Building scaffolding

Completely useless: the spire is without architectural function. It has no rentable area or structural purpose, and thus the emerging modernists considered it a sort of architectural pornography—perhaps they enjoyed it in secret. But the spire did place Walter Chrysler and architect William Van Alen in the popular pantheon.

Page 35
Looking west across the Second Avenue El toward the Empire State Building

Although an airship did drop a bundle of newspapers onto an upper deck, the mooring mast on the Empire State Building was never actually used.

Pages 36–37
Daily News Building, 42nd Street and Second Avenue

This chunky 1930 skyscraper was Raymond Hood's ultra-visionary reproach to the intricate decoration of the Chanin Building (at left) and Chrysler Building

(obscured, at center). The sophistication of the Daily News Building is evident only close up, but even so I'll take the reproached.

Page 38
Barclay-Vesey Building, 140 West Street

This Art Deco telephone building was punctured by falling steel in the collapse of the World Trade Center in 2001. On the right, the Washington Market, demolished for the Trade Center, which wrecked thousands of small businesses. Protests against it were futile.

Pages 39–43 (gatefold)
New York Life Insurance Building, northeast corner of Madison Avenue and 26th Street

Although one of those tour bus monuments (so big that people think it must be good), in architectural quality, this bloated chateau is a flight of steps down from the earlier headquarters, the sumptuous 346 Broadway. But it is great at night, with tower lighting.

Page 44
East on 42nd Street from the Chrysler Building while under construction

Tudor City in the background; the Consolidated Edison plant on the East River; the steel of the Daily News Building rising at center; but the most potent subject here is the excellent view of the Third Avenue El station in the foreground, a village of gables, with billboards, railings, and decks clearly visible.

Page 45
Southwest from the Chrysler Building while under construction

The sound of rivets must have been ringing throughout midtown in the late 1920s; the view here is interrupted by two hanging cables while work is under way on the Chrysler Building. Architects and developers everywhere were struggling with how to crown a skyscraper: To the right the Lincoln Building, at 42nd Street and Madison Avenue, has a Venetian arch appearing in steel at the top.

Page 49
1 Fifth Avenue, southeast corner of 8th Street

Another favorite "urban contrast": the skyscraper hotel-apartment by Harvey Wiley Corbett (who also designed the 1939 Tombs) rises above the proper red brick rowhouses of Washington Square.

The raised vertical bands flanking the windows, one side shadowed and dark, the other side light, are actually an illusion created by colored brick to emphasize the verticality of the building.

Pages 50-51
North on Fifth Avenue, past the Waldorf-Astoria

Flags, flags, flags—they made this section of Fifth Avenue a favorite subject for the artist Childe Hassam. Note how the slower pace and volume of traffic made pedestrians feel safe pausing in the middle of the street. Most of the buildings in this photograph are still there—it is automobile traffic that is the enemy of the urban experience. This is also the future site of the Empire State Building.

Pages 52-53
Saks Fifth Avenue, northeast corner of 50th Street and Fifth Avenue

The Landmarks Preservation Commission calls it "a handsome, but restrained and dignified neo-Renaissance style retail palazzo," but the Saks store is really just B+ commercial architecture.

By the way, John Davis, in the banner across the avenue, lost in 1924; but Smith won re-election as governor.

Page 53
The Union Club, northeast corner of 51st Street and Fifth Avenue

The photographers here capture the fading elegance of New York's cynosure men's social institutions—called "the mother of clubs" because of the many others it spawned. The soiled limestone, strange half-shadowing, and burst of commerce—with the flag of the jeweler Cartier at left—calls into question this unusual institution, which was built here in 1901 when the area was still a stronghold of the mansions of its members.

Pages 54-55
The last of the Vanderbilt mansions, northwest corner of 51st Street and Fifth Avenue

The Vanderbilts transformed this section of Fifth Avenue with a dozen great houses, beginning with this one in 1882. But within two decades they were fighting a pitched battle against traffic, hotels, stores, and even garment factories, and built unneeded mansions simply to lock up the land against commercial uses—or so they thought. By the 1910s they had surrendered, but Grace Vanderbilt, widow of Cornelius Vanderbilt III, remained at the old fort until 1942.

Page 57
Hotel President, 234 West 48th Street

The President is just a serviceable background building, but it shows that an attractive cityscape is not made up of a few bursts of capital-A architecture, but a broad fabric of assured vernacular structures: look at the simple grace of the decorative brick return on the sidewall, a nice touch of noblesse oblige. Architectural critics tend to get worked up over the major monuments of a city—but is it not really the cumulative effect of all the little things like this that make of the character of a place?

At far right, the globe lights mark the roof garden of the Astor Hotel facing Times Square.

Page 61
Ambassador Hotel, northeast corner of Park Avenue and 51st Street

A conventional 1920's apartment hotel, one of the profitable ripples spread out by the New York Central's decision to cover over its rail yards, "drawing wealth from the air" in the words of the engineer who originated the idea, William J. Wilgus.

Pages 62-63
Hotel Belleclaire, southwest corner of 77th Street and Broadway

Although damaged by storefront installations as early as the 1930s, this early Emery Roth design of 1903 was still an important part of a burp of Art Nouveau styling at the turn of the century in New York. Almost every part of the hotel shows Roth's search for a design outside classical conventions: the intricate ironwork at the roof, as good as anything on the Paris metro; the giant cascading ornamental panels in limestone flanking the window bays; the twelve-over-three pane windows; the floral ornament brought across the tops of the fourth floor windows; the wild corner turret with upended brackets.

Pages 64-65
Fred F. French Building, 551 Fifth Avenue

Built in 1927 by Fred Fillmore French, it was called "Mesopotamian" by its architect, H. Douglas Ives, with bright terra cotta and giant sunbursts on the broad north and south sides of the tower—indicating progress, according to Ives. But the critic George S. Chappell complained, "Can't the Fifth Avenue Association do something about this?"

Pages 68–69
30 Rockefeller Plaza

Ornament: A-
Architecture: C+
Vision: A+

Pages 70–73
Sunken Garden, 30 Rockefeller Plaza

Like many sunken plazas, this one was a pointless destination—until it was converted to a skating rink in 1936. At far left, the last of the Vanderbilt mansions. The Rockefellers must have mused on the passing of the Vanderbilt's architectural extravagance; although they lived just around the corner, the Baptist Rockefellers never built any big showy palace, preferring a sensible, used house on 54th off Fifth Avenue, later incorporated into the site of the Museum of Modern Art.

Page 74
Looking north on Broadway, past the Times Building at 42nd Street

It is indeed a pity the 1904 Times Building was stripped in the 1960s for the present cheesy marble-covered shaft. But far more interesting is the Heidelberg Building, just south of it with the two Camel signs at top and bottom. This peculiar structure was designed in 1909 by Henry Ives Cobb for a Missouri syndicate—in New York, out of towners tend to build well outside the norms. At first the Heidelberg was to be a thirty-story tower, but only a seven-story office building went up, with a setback tower eleven stories high, erected solely as an advertising vehicle to bring in $25,000 a year. But despite its prime location, the advertising venture failed—one advertising executive said that signs so high up could not be seen from the street, and the structure was demolished in the 1990s.

In the right distance, note the Hotel Astor, whose roof garden is also visible in the view of the Hotel President.

Page 75
The Woolworth Building, Broadway and Park Place

This 1917 terra cotta–clad structure, the tallest in the world for a decade, was the epitome of tall building technology for its time, but look . . . it still has . . . awnings! Much is made of the architect Cass Gilbert's neo-Gothic "Cathedral of Commerce," but is the building really such a masterpiece? What else might another architect have done? This does not depart so far from the norm—would any building of this height on this site not be so canonized?

As a counterpoint in architectural taste, the General Post Office at lower left (just beyond the cupola of City Hall) was magnificent when it was built in the 1870s, but considered an excrescence by the early twentieth century, in part for detracting from the supposed pristine verdure of City Hall Park. The Post Office got its comeuppance in 1939 when it was demolished—but would its destruction have generated protests in our own time?

Pages 76–77
Chrysler Building, basement room

Was Hydrozone just a racket—like the inexplicable spread of bottled water in our own time?

Page 80
Fisk Tire Building, 250 West 57th Street, from Broadway to Eighth Avenue

The Fisk Building was probably the biggest vehicle-related structure to go up on Automobile Row, and a demure work for a simple office building, designed by Carrere & Hastings with Shreve & Lamb.

Sometimes the interest is all in the margins: in this case, the skylit spaces at the top of the Fisk; the neat little garage building at lower left; the play lot at lower right, owned by William Randolph Hearst (and site of the present Hearst Building), at times used as a tennis court; and the column stubs projecting from the roof of the Colonnade Building, at lower right—built to three stories in 1921. A few years after this photograph it was expanded upwards to twenty-six stories.

Page 81
American Radiator Building, 40 West 40th Street, seen from Bryant Park

The striking black and gold American Radiator Building, by the ebullient architect Raymond Hood, was of black brick topped with gold-colored masonry, nominally evoking the glowing embers of a fire. Special floodlighting made the building "one of the sights of the city" at night, said the magazine *American Architect*.

Pages 84–85
Looking northwest from the Chrysler Building to the New York Central Building, 230 Park Avenue, at 46th Street

The thiry-four-story New York Central Building, straddling Park between 45th and 46th Streets, was the grandest of the buildings erected over the New York Central's rail yards. Built in 1928, it includes one of the best auto rides in New York, a looping series of tight turns through the twin tunnels of 230 Park, past the

Pan Am Building, around Grand Central Terminal, and back on the other side if you choose. It is marred only by the appalling filth covering the interior of the high, vaulted spaces. The lacy top of 230 Park is one of the sights of the city—especially if seen from nearby, at its own level.

Look also to right of center, the top of 466 Lexington Avenue—like most in the city, the parapet wall is just a sham, hiding nothing behind it except its own supports.

Pages 86–91 (gatefold)
The Circle Building, west side of Columbus Avenue

Built in 1914 by William Randolph Hearst, a big believer in this section of town, but his own visions were not realized. Examine the streets: how safe for pedestrians they were at an earlier time, with vehicles and pedestrians cooperating in a stately minuet. By assigning exclusive use of the roadways to motor vehicles, we have lost a huge chunk of public space, leaving only tiny marginal strips of pedestrian safety, with the roadways themselves transformed into kill zones.

As the billboards suggest, this was part of Automobile Row, which started with carriage factories in Longacre (now Times) Square and stretched up to 70th Street and Broadway until deflating down to 57th Street and Eleventh Avenue.

Pages 92–93
Miller Highway, south across the rail yards at 72nd Street

What is now usually called the West Side Highway matched perfectly, in its mechanistic design, the industrial character of the waterfront, a mixture of car ferry terminals, loading docks, and transfer stations. Now the railroad in the foreground has been replaced by a string of apartment houses built by Donald Trump, and the pier at right has become a park. From it, on September 11, 2001, it was possible to see the Trade Center fall.

Pages 96–97
South past the Cathedral of St. John the Divine, from 113th Street and Amsterdam Avenue

This epic photograph captures the breadth of the city, but also contains details like rooftop laundry drying racks and a sunbather. The diagonal property line at right (a leftover from an old lane, but later ratified by buildings) is repeated farther south, visible as a whitish wall directly below the Empire State Building.

The scaffolding on the left is evidence of the end of construction of the Cathedral, which was started in the 1890s—by the 1940s the idea of an urban cathedral in the Gothic style seemed, at best, silly.

The north skylights at center are the temporary studios of the National Academy of Design, which sought to build a grand headquarters and join Columbia, St. John, and the other institutions, but had to settle for its present townhouse on Fifth Avenue near 90th Street.

Pages 98–99
North across the Columbia University campus

The old Low Library dome is at right center, the neo-Gothic Riverside Church is at left center, and the George Washington Bridge is in the distance. More a roofscape than a cityscape, the exact composition of this photograph seems chosen more for the access point than for anything else.

Page 100
Pythian Temple, 135 West 70th Street

This $2 million fraternal headquarters was designed by theater architect Thomas Lamb with brilliantly colored terra cotta and an Egyptian-style colonnade at the top, and thirteen separate lodge rooms for the constituent members of the Knights of Pythias.

Pages 104–107
Panhellenic House, northeast corner of 49th Street and First Avenue

Originally conceived as a hotel for sorority members, the Panhellenic went up in 1928, designed by the modernist John Mead Howells. It was organized by a group of social register women headed by Emily Hepburn, who had also promoted the historical restoration of the Theodore Roosevelt house at 28 East 20th Street only a few years before, so the Art Deco styling of this building is of particular interest. Howells said he had the brick executed with tinted mortar set in joints flush with the surface to try to make the building appear sculpted from a single block of clay. The Panhellenic foundered shortly after the crash of 1929 and was soon converted to a conventional hotel.

Page 124
North past 30 Sutton Place at 58th Street, to the Queensboro (59th Street) Bridge

The new Sutton Place of the 1920s was conceived as a picturesque blending of the industrial waterfront with elite co-ops and town houses. Here Peyser & Patzig build on that theme, incorporating Rosario Candela's 30 Sutton Place apartment building (and 25, barely visible at right), the two brick chimneys, and the spiky design of the 59th Street Bridge's striking cantilever.

ACKNOWLEDGMENTS

Thank you, Margaret Kaplan, for believing in my vision of sharing this extraordinary collection. Without your enthusiasm and support I don't think this book would have become a reality. What a pleasure it has been to work with the Abrams team. Deborah Aaronson's sharp critiques and wise direction, along with Miko McGinty's eye for layout, made the process smooth and fun. A special thank you to Christopher Gray for his continued encouragement and fabulous contributions to this work.

I am also grateful to Ford Peatross and Maricia Battle of the Library of Congress for their kind cooperation during my visits to access my gifted collection. My "computer mavens," Thomas Oh and Matthew Stravitz, have been terrific, lending their expertise to the monumental amount of scanning and cataloging required for this project. I am grateful to my wife, Amy, and our daughter, Alison, who came through again, helping me along each step of the way. And finally, a special thank you to New York City!

Project Director: Margaret L. Kaplan

Editor: Deborah Aaronson

Designer: Miko McGinty

Production Managers: Stanley Redfern and Norman Watkins

Library of Congress Cataloging-in-Publication Data

New York, Empire City, 1920–1945 / [compiled by] David Stravitz ;
with an essay by Christopher Gray.
    p. cm.
 Includes bibliographical references and index.
 ISBN 0-8109-5011-1
 1. Architectural photography–New York (State)–New
York–History–20th century. 2. New York (N.Y.)–Buildings, structures,
etc.–Pictorial works. 3. New York (N.Y.)–History–Pictorial works.
I. Stravitz, David, 1940– II. Title.

TR659.N47 2004
779'.99747'1–dc22

2004005962

Printed and bound in Singapore

10 9 8 7 6 5 4 3 2 1

Harry N. Abrams, Inc.
100 Fifth Avenue
New York, N.Y. 10011
www.abramsbooks.com

Abrams is a subsidiary of

LA MARTINIÈRE